Anonymous

Lights of the Legislature of 1874

Anonymous

Lights of the Legislature of 1874

ISBN/EAN: 9783337253714

Printed in Europe, USA, Canada, Australia, Japan

Cover: Foto ©Suzi / pixelio.de

More available books at **www.hansebooks.com**

Lights of the Legislature

OF

1874.

WRITTEN BY

A REPORTER OF THE ASSEMBLY.

ALBANY, N. Y.:

THE ARGUS COMPANY, PRINTERS.

1874.

INTRODUCTORY.

Perched upon a high desk in the front of the Assembly chamber during the session now at its close, it has been the privilege of the writer to look upon the law-makers of the State during their official term, and to form conclusions of their several distinctive merits. In the spare moments which have come to him during the three months sitting he has jotted down hasty pen pictures of those who have distinguished themselves, in his opinion, during the session, and who can be regarded as lights of the Legislature. He has perhaps looked wholly on the sunny side of human nature, and not allowed the acid to preponderate over the sweetness; but his praise has the merit of candor and honesty, and is only tendered to those who, in his humble judgment, deserve it. The "hundred days" had come and gone before these sketches were given form, in order that no false statements be made, for a Greek proverb was remembered which says: "Praise the fineness of the day when it is ended, praise a woman when you have known her, a sword when you have proved it, a maiden after she is married, the ice when you have crossed it, and the liquor after it is drunk,"—and to this the occupant of the high desk adds, a Legislator at the expiration of his term. In these half-hundred brief sketches, none have been inspired or written by the subjects. Some have asked that privilege, not reflecting that the breath of self-eulogy soils the face of the speaker, even as the censer is dimmed by the smoke of its own perfume. They do not appear within these pages, which but expresses the opinions of a disinterested "Looker on in Vienna."

ASSEMBLY CHAMBER.
ALBANY, N. Y., *April* 25, 1874.

Lights of the Legislature.

SPEAKER HUSTED.

Probably the best Speaker that ever presided over the Assembly is the Hon. James W. Husted, of Westchester, who has this year been honored with this position. Certainly he is the peer of any of his predecessors, the superior of many, and will retire the present week from his high station, with the approbation of every member, and the satisfactory approval for his efforts, from the entire people of the State. He has shown, during the session, now at its close, unflinching integrity, and the most straightforward conduct; while his polished manner and innumerable graces of mind and heart, have won the friendship and esteem of all the members. Quick as a flash, universally correct in his rulings, courteous and affable at all times, he has been the ideal speaker, and to him is almost wholly due the credit of the Assembly adjourning one month earlier this year than last. General Husted was born in the county he represents. During the latter part of the year 1833 he studied at Yale, graduated with high honors, and afterward studied law and was admitted to the Bar in 1857.

Mr. Husted has held numerous local offices as well as State, such as School Commissioner for Westchester County in 1858, and in 1860 Deputy Superintendent of the State Insurance Department. Since 1862 he has been Harbor Master of the City of New York, and until recently was Deputy Captain of the Port. He was first elected to the Assembly Chamber in 1868, since which time he has been re-elected

1*

every year.   His record, during those sessions, is so well
known as not to require to be repeated in these pages.
General Husted is a prominent member of the Masonic
Fraternity, having reached the highest order and held the
rank of D. D. G. M. for several years.   In 1873 he was nominated by Governor Dix to be Major-General of the Fifth
Division of the National Guard, and was immediately con-
firmed by the Senate.

FRANKLIN A. ALBERGER.

The champion of Buffalo and of Western New York is
found in the person of the honorable gentleman from Erie,
Franklin A. Alberger, the Chairman in the Assembly of that
most important Committee on Canals.   Mr. Alberger is prominently a light of the Legislature ; possessing a great deal of
force of character and practical ability to perform his legislative duties ably and effectively.   Few men in the chamber
are more prominent than he.   Of a commanding presence
and pleasing address, his speeches, which are eminently stir-
ring and forcible, are listened to with eager attention.   He
is also a skilled and effective debater, and keenly alive to the
welfare of his immediate constituents.   This was remarkably
displayed the other day, when Mr. Alberger moved than an
appropriation of $150,000 be inserted in the Supply Bill for
the Buffalo Asylum.   The committee had reported but ten
thousand for that institution and Gen. Batcheller, with other
leading men, strongly opposed the appropriation, when Mr.
Alberger arose, and, in a speech illustrated with statistics,
and delivered with rare oratorical power, he demanded the
appropriation, and made so powerful a plea therefor as to
carry the House with him and to secure to Buffalo, so far as
the Assembly was concerned, the appropriation.   It was a
crushing defeat to his opponents, and manifested plainly the
influence of Mr. Alberger.   The subject of these remarks was
born in Baltimore, Md., in January, 1825, but when quite
young became a resident of Buffalo, of which city he has
been repeatedly alderman and once mayor.   Mr. Alberger

has been elected to the Assembly four consecutive terms. He has held the office of Canal Commissioner for six years, and now has a reputation extending from Montauk Point to his own city. He is married, and socially, is one of the most genial and cultured gentlemen that has come to Albany this winter.

THOMAS G. ALVORD.

Under the great chandelier of the Chamber, in the very choicest seat—which was extended to him at the beginning of the session, as a mark of respect and esteem—sits the patriarch of the House, " Honest Tom Alvord," of Syracuse. He represents the Independent element of the Legislature, and bears his honors unblushingly. No man so well as he, has the faculty of putting things in so happy and convincing a style as "Old Salt." He speaks fluently and well, is never verbose, but always practical, and during this session has, more than once, extricated the House out of a maze of difficulties by his ready and earnest talk. Mr. Alvord has had many bitter words said about him during the present session by the press of the metropolis, owing to his relentless cutting up of those editors, who will condemn a measure without fully understanding its aim and purport. But as not a word of suspicion has been uttered against his good name, Mr. Alvord has rather gained in celebrity by those one-sided attacks, which may do him more good than harm. It is, perhaps, unnecessary for us to discuss at length the many personal attributes of Mr. Alvord ; he is too well and favorably known for that, but we know that he is a man of the most genial manner, generous instincts and numerous graces of character, possessing most of those qualities of mind and heart which win popularity. As a Legislator he takes the front rank, and his words at all times commands the complete attention of the House, while his oratorical ability is marvelously excellent. Mr. Alvord was born in the county he now represents, in December, 1810. He was educated at Yale, graduating with high honors from that venerab'e institution in 1828. He studied law for two years and was admitted to the Bar. Essentially a man of the people, he has been repeatedly honored by them. First elected to the Legislature in 1844, he served in that body during the years 1858, 1862, 1864, 1870, 1871, 1872, 1874. He was Speaker of the House in 1858 and 1864. He was also elected Lieutenant-Governor in 1864, on the ticket with Governor Fenton, serving during the years 1865–6. The Senate never had a more impartial President than he. He was a member of the Constitutional Convention in 1867–8. Thus can we see how brilliant a light is the gentleman from Onondaga.

Mr. BATCHELLER,

Of Saratoga.—The Premier of the House, the Chancellor of the Exchequer and the spokesman for the majority, Gen. George S. Batcheller, occupies in the present Assembly a position of peculiar honor and responsibility. He has shown himself well worthy of the substantial compliments lavished upon him, for, as Chairman of the Committee on Ways and Means, he has distinguished himself greatly by sending to the Senate the "cleanest" Supply Bill that ever passed the lower House of the Legislature. This is high praise indeed, but it is just and will show better than anything we can say, the fitness of Gen. Batcheller for the position he occupies. Saratoga county is represented admirably this year in both its members. This year few sections have two such able men to look after their interests, as the subject of this sketch and his colleague, Mr. West. Gen. Batcheller is a natural talker, fluent and ready upon any subject. He is urbane and pleasant in his address, carrying with him an atmosphere of gayety and good cheer, treating all with the deference a gentleman invariably pays to those he comes in contact with. As a Legislator he has proved himself to be able and wonderfully efficient, and but adds this year to a reputation already great and honorable.

Mr. Batcheller was born in Batchellerville, Saratoga County, July 25, 1837, and is descended from somewhat an illustrious family; he was educated at Harvard College and shortly afterward was admitted to the Bar and soon rose to eminence in his profession. In 1858 he was elected to the Assembly from the same district now represented by him, and was again elected in 1872 and 1873. Mr. B. is entitled to the rank of General both on account of his appointment on Gov. Fenton's staff as Inspector-General, as well as for his services in the war.

Mr. BEEBE,

Of Sullivan—Sitting at the extreme right of the Speaker's desk is George Monroe Beebe, the real leader of the opposition in the Assembly, and a member universally respected; who during this session has added new laurels to his already brilliant reputation. Mr. Beebe is a positive man—no one who can look upon the earnest intelligent features of the gentleman from Sullivan but can discover that. His clear and quick perceptions, sound judgment and practical common sense impress, most forcibly, all who come in contact with him. As a citizen he is universally esteemed and respected, while his kindly nature always displayed in an unostentatious manner has endeared him to those toward whom it has been exercised. As a lawyer, Mr. Beebe occupies a high rank in his profession. Firm as a rock when battling for the right, his mind is unswayed by extraneous circumstances. His integrity is acknowledged by all, and has never, so far as we know, been questioned. Mr. Beebe is a Democrat of the Jeffersonian school. He is a Democrat from principle, and his wisdom and counsels are often consulted by party leaders. No one in the present House can make a speech so commanding and eloquent as he, and if a measure receives his approval and advice much is accomplished from its passage. He is the popular Democratic leader to whom all the young members of that party go for advice. He is a kind, worthy, estimable gentleman, who looks at times, cross and unapproachable, but he is the opposite of that, and although a remarkably able man, whose presence would adorn the Senate Chamber or our Congressional Halls, yet is he as kindly and courteous to the page boy at his side as to the Governor of the State.

JOHN P. BADGER.

Mr. Badger, who is now in his second term in the House, is sustaining the excellent record that he made last year, when he was a member of the Committees on State Prisons, Federal Relations and Engrossed Bills, and the Speaker taking into account his many Legislative qualities assigned him this year to the Chairmanship of the Committee on State Prisons, and member of the Committees on Grievances and Sub-Comittee of the Whole, in which capacities he has shown himself to be a hard and untiring worker. Mr. Badger has, on several times, addressed the House on local measures effectively and although he cannot be termed an orator he has a pleasant delivery and what he says, is curt and to the purpose. He is invariably to be found in his seat, zealously watching the interests of his constituents and of the State at large.

John Peaslee Badger, was born in Ossipee, Carroll county, N. H., August 3, 1834, but his parents removing to this State, he received his education in the common schools of Franklin County, and finally graduating from the Albany Law School, he was admitted to the Bar in 1871, and at once commenced the practice of his profession.

Mr. Badger early allied himself to the Republican party, and in 1870, and 1872, he was elected a member of the Board of Supervisors for his town. He was elected to his present seat by a majority of 1,067 over Mr. Baker Stevens, Democrat.

He is now regarded as one of the strongest men upon the floor.

BERNARD BIGLIN.

This gentleman, who represents the Eighteenth district of New York city, is now on his second term, having so far pleased his constituents last year as to be re-elected by a plurality of 556 over two formidable opponents. Mr. Biglin was born in Pennsylvania, in 1841, of Irish parents, and received his education in the common schools. Removing to New York at an early age he learned the trade of a brass moulder; but soon after completing his apprenticeship he was appointed to a position as Inspector in the New York Custom-house, which he held for three years. He was afterward appointed Inspector in the Internal Revenue Department, where he served for four years.

Mr. Biglin, who is a follower in the Republican ranks, has, for a number of years, been associated with New York politics, and taken an active part in the primaries and conventions of his party, both county and State.

Mr. Biglin has been most active in the discharge of his duties as Chairman of the Committee on Commerce and Navigation, and has been very punctual in his attendance at the House, and ever wakeful to the interests of his constituents. As a speaker he is distinct and brief, but he seldom takes the floor, except on matters that concern the interests of his constituents.

EUGENE D. BERRI.

The County of Kings has sent many excellent representatives to the Assembly for the last ten years, but in no case have they sent one who has done more justice to his constituents and the citizens in general than Mr. Eugene D. Berri, who is now closing his second term.

Mr. Berri was born in Buffalo in 1836, of English parents, and accompanied them on their removal to Brooklyn, where he received his education, chiefly in the public schools, but it may safely be said that he is a self-educated man. At an early age he embarked in the carpet business, and is now a member of one of the largest establishments of that kind in Brooklyn. During the Rebellion he served for a short time as First Lieutenant in the 132d Regiment, New York Volunteers, and performed active service at Suffolk, N. C.

In politics Mr. Berri is a Republican, but although he has always been interested in political matters, he did not accept any office until he entered the Assembly in 1872, when he was elected over Thomas W. Adams by a majority of 1,858, on which occasion he made an honorable record. Last fall he was elected to his present seat by a majority of 2,277 over Chalmers M. Benson, and is credited to the Chairmanship of the Committee on Expenditures of the Executive Department, and is a member of those on Insurance and Banks, and he has done noble work both in the Committees and in the House, being constant in his attendance.

Mr. Berri frequently takes the floor on matters pertaining to his County and touching the interests of his constituents. As a speaker he is fluent and distinct, but his speeches are generally brief and to the point.

ARTHUR F. BROWN.

Directly in front of the Speaker's desk, always in his seat and closely watching the manner of legislation, sits a pleasant-faced gentleman, who we find to be Mr. Arthur F. Brown of Oneida, one of the most reliable, careful and prudent members of the present Legislature. During the session, now at its close, Mr. Brown has made for himself a reputation, among the thoughtful men of the House, as a member always to be relied upon for his vote on honest legislation. Listening carefully to the debates upon leading questions, in which he seldom takes a part, he acts according to the dictates of his own judgment, which are generally correct. Not to be cajoled into a vote which shall not represent the real interests of the people, he is a gentleman held in high esteem by the Speaker and other leaders of the party with which Mr. Brown acts. No man in the Assembly Chamber this winter has gained for himself a finer reputation for consistency and honor, than the member of whom we speak. Upright and honorable in all his dealings, faithful to the will of his constituency, and possessed of a well-balanced mind, the people of Oneida County have reason to be proud of their quiet but working member. Mr. Brown was born in the county he represents. There he has lived for a lifetime, and been intrusted with several prominent offices, one of which was Supervisor, and when a voter has recorded himself upon the side of equality and justice. A Republican, earnest and unfaltering, a vigorous advocate for the prosecution of the late war, and a man of practical every-day common sense. Mr. Brown is one of those men who could not fail to make the excellent record as a Legislator he has. In the present Assembly he is a member of three important committees, on Claims, Roads and Bridges and Indian Affairs.

FRANCIS B. BREWER.

Close by the aisle leading from the lobby to the chamber sits a somewhat portly gentleman, whose *tout ensemble* would not fail to bring him to the notice of even a casual observer. His cheerful florid countenance is an index to his mind, and his long flowing beard gives him a venerable appearance. This gentleman we recognize as Mr. Francis B. Brewer, who is now representing the County of Chautauqua for the second time. He comes from good old Revolutionary stock, and was born in Keene, N. H., where he received a good liberal education, and afterward entered Dartmouth College, from whence he graduated in 1843, and then pursued the medical studies attached to the same college, where, obtaining a doctor's diploma, he practiced his profession for five years, when he entered the lumbering business at Oil Creek, in Pennsylvania. Having been most successful in his ventures in the oil regions, Mr. Brewer removed to Westfield, in Chautauqua County, where he now resides, and is interested in extensive mercantile pursuits. He has, repeatedly, been the recipient

2

of political honors from his fellow-citizens, by whom he is held in high esteem. Last year, as member of the Committee on Ways and Means, he did most effectual service in reducing the expenditures, and this session he is retained on the same committee, and is also Chairman of Petitions of Aliens, and member of Committee on Charitable and Religious Societies. Mr. Brewer, who is a Republican in politics, is a strong adherent to his party, a man of decided ability and much practical good sense; he is quick to understand the bearings of every question which he is called upon to consider, and therefore possesses qualities invaluable in the Legislator. He has frequently taken the floor and expressed his views on various knotty questions, which he does in plain yet graceful language. Dr. Brewer has been very punctual in his attendance at the House, and attentive to the interests of his constituents.

WATERS W. BRAMAN.

Directly to the left of the Speaker, can at all times be found in his seat, the careful and hard-working member from West Troy. A gentleman of pleasant manners and incorruptible character, possessing, in a large degree, those qualities so essential to the able Legislator. Mr. Braman is eminently qualified to be classed among the lights of the Assembly of 1874. He is at all times against all corrupt schemes, and his record will bear the searching scrutiny of his constituents.

Mr. Braman repeatedly has taken the floor, and although he cannot be termed an orator, in the strict sense of the word, he expresses his views pointedly and logically.

Mr. Waters W. Braman was born in Troy, N. Y., April 20, 1840, but his parents dying when he was but a child, he was brought up by his uncle, Mr. Waters W. Whipple of Troy. Receiving a good sound English education in the common school and high school of his native town, at the age of twenty he became a member of the firm of Belknap & Braman, lumber dealers, but at the outbreak of the Rebellion he at once went to the front and earned an excellent

army record, retiring with the rank of Major. At the close
of the war he married Margaret J. Getty, of West Troy, and
became an active member of the lumber firm of W. W.
Whipple & Co., which he retains at the present time. In
politics the Major is an active Republican, but his political
history is briefly told. He is at the present time a trustee of
the village of West Troy, and, outside of his present position
in the House, he has held no other office.

WILLIAM L. BOSTWICK.

Mr. Bostwick, who enters the Assembly Chamber for the
first time as a Legislator, was born in Enfield, N. Y., March
15, 1837, but removed to Ithaca in 1863, where he is largely
connected with the mercantile interests of that town. In
1860 and 1861, he was elected Supervisor, on the Republican
ticket, from Enfield, and was Chairman of that Board, from
Ithaca, in 1867, in which capacities he made a good record.
He was also a delegate from the Twenty-seventh Congressional
District to the Philadelphia Republican Convention which
nominated Gen. Grant in 1872.

He was elected to his present seat, by a majority of 274,
over Charles W. Bates, Democrat, and William Hanford,
Temperance. He is Chairman of the Committee on Education, and a member of Committee on Public Printing and
Sub-Committee of the Whole.

Mr. Bostwick has been most indefatigable in his duties
during the session ; always in his seat, he watches closely all
the proceedings, but his chief exertions have been in behalf
of educational measures, with which subjects he is thoroughly
at home and conversant. Possessing a clear and distinct
enunciation, his arguments are listened to with much attention by the members of the House. His words are uttered
with a graceful force and precision, while he invariably
speaks to the point at issue. When an especially important
bill is up for consideration, he prepares his speeches with
much deliberation, but even when addressing the House

extemporaneously he is certainly entitled to a foremost place
in the oratorical ranks.   His speech, in nominating the Rev.
Dr. Upson for the office of Regent of the University, was a
masterly production, and, on several occasions, the House
has been cognizant of his ability, in several sharp contests.
A bright political future appears in store for the worthy
member from Tompkins County.

GEORGE W. CHADWICK.

This gentleman who represents the First district of Oneida
County, was born in Paris, in the County of Oneida, June 16,
1825, of Anglo-American parents, his father having emigrated
to this country in 1812.   He received a good, sound common
school and academic education and early embarked in the
manufacturing business with his father, who, at his death, left
the whole business to him, and, at the present time, Mr. C. is
the sole proprietor of one of the largest manufacturing
establishments in the county, situated at Chadwick's Mills.
He employs 150 hands and is greatly beloved by his opera-
tives, having done all in his power to enhance their welfare
and comfort.   He married in 1855, Miss Mary Wrigley, of
Lancashire, England, and has one son.

In politics, Mr. C. is a Republican, and has held several
positions.   During the war he was elected Supervisor for the
County of Oneida, for three successive terms and executed
the duties of that office, which were at that time most onerous,
with much success and ability.

In 1871 he was elected to the Assembly by a majority of
684 over Colonel Cooke, Democrat, during which session he
made for himself an excellent record.   He was elected to his
present seat by a majority of nearly 800, over Harvey Talcott,
Democrat, and is Chairman of the Committee on Civil Divisions, and a member of the Committee on Railroads.

Mr. Chadwick lays no claim to oratory; but he is entitled to
a prominent notice in these pages on account of the superior
judgment he has exercised in the discharge of his duties.

Invariably in his seat he watches the interests of his district with the strictest attention and has been most successful in passing what measures he has taken in hand.

The most important bill touching the interests of Utica, that has been passed this session, is the Utica Fire and Police Commission Bill which was introduced by Senator Lowery in the Upper House. Mr. Chadwick was most assiduous in endeavoring to find out the true wishes of the citizens of Utica in respect to the bill, and it was not until after he was satisfied in his own mind, that he urged the passage of the bill.

Although the New York Times wrote a most scurrilous article on the members of the Committee on Railroads, the writer exonerated Mr. Chadwick, who is also a member of that committee from any charges, and said that his honesty and integrity could not be questioned. This is indeed, a high compliment emanating from such a paper as the Times.

STEPHEN J. COLAHAN.

Although but in his thirty-second year, Mr. Colahan has made a splendid political record. He has been a delegate to nearly all the State and judiciary conventions for the past six years, and was a member, in 1867 and 1868, of the Constitutional Commission, of which body, although the young-est, he was a prominent member and a strong upholder of Democratic principles. His speech in opposition to the clause prohibiting the sale of intoxicating liquors, and one in favor of regulating the sale and the dispensing of drugs, were so effective that they were republished in pamphlet form, and the State Medical Board indorsed his views and tendered him a banquet. Mr. Colahan is a highly educated man, having received the advantages of Fordham College, after which, graduating from the law department of the New York University, he commenced the practice of the law in Brooklyn, and in 1871 was appointed chief clerk of the City Court of that city. In 1872 he was a candidate for Congress

2*

from the Fourth district, but was defeated by a small majority by General Crook, a Republican, and with whom he was formerly associated in law business. Mr. C. was elected to the present Assembly by a majority of forty over Mr. Cochen, Republican and Patrick J. Gleason, Independent. He is an active member of the Committees on Judiciary and Privileges and Elections, and has only been absent from his seat in the House, when the special duties of his position at home called him away.

As an orator Mr. Colaban ranks high, possessing a full and pleasing voice, he puts forth his views and arguments distinctly and forcibly; the utmost silence prevails, and the attention of the House is riveted when he takes the floor. Among the principal measures that he has advocated, are the following: The Fourth street bill; the bill to form a Park in Brooklyn; the Ferry Reform bill; the Trust Company of Brooklyn; the bill to amend the Excise Law, so as to give alleged offenders the privilege of a trial by jury, and a bill in favor of Mr. Milburne, an alien. He also took the floor against the Academy Appropriation, and in a somewhat lengthy but extremely logical speech, he was partly instrumental in having that item stricken out of the Appropriation Bill. An excellent record during the present session, he has certainly made.

JAMES DALY.

This gentleman, who represents the Fourteenth district of New York city, is but a novice in political honors, but a bright career is predicted for him. He is a native of Westmeath, Ireland, where he was born in 1843, and where he received a high collegiate education, having been originally intended for the church, but in 1864, emigrating to this country, he engaged in mercantile pursuits. Mr. Daly is a Democrat, but was one of the foremost to aid in the overthrow of the corrupt Tammany ring. He was elected, by a majority of 636, over Carl Schmedler, Republican, and John Murphy, Democrat.

Mr. Daly has been most punctual in his attendance in the House, and the very first day of the session he inaugurated his entry as a Legislator by a powerful speech in behalf of the unemployed of the City of New York, and has frequently addressed the House on important questions pertaining to the interests of his constituents.

As an orator, he stands in the foremost rank, and when he rises he is sure to command the attention of the House, he has a strong mellow voice with a peculiar, but pleasing accent, and his speeches, which are wrapped in appropriate classical language, denote the high culture of his mind.

Mr. Daly is a working member of the Committees on Charitable and Religious Societies and Trade and Manufactures.

AUGUSTUS DENNISTON.

Mr. Denniston, member from Orange County, though quite a young man, has earned for himself an excellent political record, this being his second term in the House. Almost from boyhood he has been associated with politics, for he has invariably attended all the primary conventions, and when old enough was sent as a delegate to various political bodies. He was elected to the present Assembly by a majority of 291 over James W. Miller, of Newburgh, a prominent Democrat. Mr. Denniston has been credited to the Chairmanship of the Committee on Two-thirds and Three-fifths Bills, and is a member of the important Committees on Railroads and Charitable and Religious Societies, and has proved himself to be a valuable acquisition in the Committee-room as well as in the House, on the practical details of legislation. He has several times joined in the debates and made brief but sharp speeches. He is a keen observer, quick of manner, and can easily determine the true nature of a bill at a glance.

Augustus Denniston was born at Blooming Grove, Orange County, May 25, 1842, and received a high education, at home, from tutors. He went to the front, at an early stage of the rebellion, as Quartermaster of the 124th Regiment, New York Volunteers, where he made a good record. Mr. D. occupies his time in managing the large estate left him by his father.

HARVEY G. EASTMAN.

To the left of the Speaker's desk, and directly under the clock, sits a gentleman of marked individuality, at least, one who cannot escape the notice of even a stranger to the legislative halls, for those sharp features and restless eyes must command attention. Mr. Eastman, member for Poughkeepsie, who is the occupant of that seat, was born in Marshall, Oneida County, November 16, 1832, and received but a scanty education, except what he taught himself; and it is owing to this want that his idea was first started to form a school which should aim to give young men the practical business knowledge which is not generally taught in common schools and academies. And although he commenced with but one pupil and met with but adversity and discouragement, yet, by the energy and indomitable perseverance which is characteristic of the man, he has built up the largest Business College in the United States—his pupils numbering 1,600. Poughkeepsie may well be proud of such a man. Mr. Eastman, who is a Republican in politics, has been the recipient of many public trusts from his fellow-citizens. He is now serving his second term as Chief Magistrate of Poughkeepsie, and also his second session in the Assembly Chamber, having been elected in 1871.

For eight years he has held the office of State Commissioner of Public Charities. In appearance, Mr. Eastman is a true specimen of an American, a man of generous impulses, genial disposition and courteous address, he has made a favorable impression here this winter, and is very popular among his fellow-members. He constantly takes the floor, and expresses his views distinctly and fluently. The Rapid Transit Scheme for New York city, introduced by him, made quite an excitement in the House, owing to the Chairman of the Railroad Committee failing to report the same in due season, which elicited an inflammatory article from the New York Times against the said committee. Mr. Eastman has discharged the arduous duties as Chairman of Cities with much tact, ability and unyielding impartiality, and has also been an active member of the Committees on Grievances and State Charitable Institutions, as well as Chairman of the important Committee on Cities.

HAMILTON FISH, Jr.

The subject of this sketch was born in Albany, April 17, 1849, during the period his father was Governor of the State. He was educated at Columbia College, New York City, where he graduated with honor, and, after acting as private secretary to his father, in the State Department, for two years, he entered the law school attached to Columbia College, and, in 1873, he graduated and was admitted to the Bar, and commenced the practice of his profession in New York City. When Governor Dix was elected, he was appointed aide-de-camp on his staff, with the rank of Colonel.

Mr. Fish, on attaining his majority, allied himself with the Republican party, and during the exciting Presidential campaign of 1872 he was Chairman of the Putnam County Republican Committee, and also a delegate to the State Convention at Utica, in which capacities he did great service to his party. He was elected to his seat in the Assembly by a majority of 431 over Saxton Smith, a powerful Democratic opponent.

Although the youngest member of the House, Mr. Fish was appointed, by the Speaker, Chairman of the Committee on State Charitable Institutions, and member of the Committees on Cities and Militia, and he has been most active and attentive in the discharge of his duties in the different committees, and is never absent from his seat in the House.

The Colonel makes no pretentions as an orator, but he has, on several occasions, taken part in debates, and has shown that his views are solid and well considered. He has passed several important local measures, and has taken great interest in matters pertaining to New York city, being a member of the important Committee on Cities.

ALONZO H. FARRAR.

Mr. Farrar is, indeed, a shining light of the Assembly of 1874, and no young man ever entered on a political career with brighter prospects. He was born in Middletown, Vt., March 29, 1843, and after receiving a good sound education at Fort Edward Institute and Burton Seminary, Manchester, Vt., he entered the Albany Law School, where he graduated with honors, and was admitted to the bar in 1864. He commenced the practice of law in Kinderhook, Columbia County, and is now recognized as one of the most powerful and brilliant members of the legal profession in Columbia County. He soon attached himself to the Republican party, and early took a deep and warm interest in politics, but did not accept any office until he was nominated to his present position by the Republican party, when he was elected by a majority of 307 over Mr. Peter Mesick, a popular Democrat. He has been a hard working member on the Committees on Judiciary, Grievances and Local and Special Laws, and has been very punctual in his attendance in the House.

Although a perfect novice in legislative affairs, Mr. Farrar at once entered into his duties with all the ability and confidence of an old Legislator. His maiden speech, in opposition to the Proposed Amendment to the Fifth Article of the Constitution, at once placed him in the foremost ranks of orators and entitled him to the notice of the whole House. His speech in favor of Compulsory Education is recognized as the finest of the session, and his remarks on the death of Senator Sumner proved him to have no superior as an orator in the Assembly; for although several eloquent and well prepared addresses were delivered on the occasion, Mr. Farrar's was the only one that was not prepared and read, but delivered on the spur of the moment.

Commanding a full and pleasant voice, he expresses his views in classical and appropriate language, and his arguments, based on common sense and good judgment, rarely fail to reach their mark. A bright future is predicted for the young member from Columbia County.

GEORGE A. GOSS.

Mr. Goss may now be termed an old Legislator, although comparatively a young man, this being his third term in the Assembly. He was born in Pittsford, N. Y., March 3d, 1834, where he has lived ever since, and he received his education in the common and union district school. On arriving at the age of twenty-one he associated himself with the Republican party, and early took an active part in politics by becoming a member of the County Central Committee. He has held several important town offices, and, in 1871, he was elected to the Assembly from Monroe County, and in 1872 was re-elected over Richard D. Cole, Democrat, by a majority of 322, when he served as Chairman of the Committee on Expenditures of the Executive Department, and member of the Committees on Villages and Education, and when he earned for himself a good record. He was elected to his present seat by a majority of 385 over S. Hatch Gould, Democrat; and this year he discharges the duties of Chairman of the Committee on Villages and member of Committees on Commerce and Navigation and Sub-Committee of the Whole. He has been very attentive and assiduous in his duties and punctual in his attendance at the House, and is a general favorite with the members.

Mr. Goss does not rank as an orator, nor does he claim to be one, but what he has to say is short and weighty. He has taken the floor on several occasions during the session, and his arguments seem to influence the members considerably.

WILLIAM C. HAZELTON.

The County of Seneca is represented this year by one of the finest-looking men in the Assembly. Tall, commanding in person, and possessing an easy, gentlemanly address, Mr. Hazelton cannot fail to attract attention in whatever society he may be in. He was born at Ulysses, Tompkins county, September 1, 1835. and after receiving a good common-school and academic education, he took a liking for the legal profession, and studied law with Dana & Beers at Ithaca, and was admitted to the Bar in 1857, and is now enjoying a very lucrative practice at Ovid.

As a Democrat, Mr. Hazelton has been an unswerving defender of its principles, and he has always taken a deep interest in the politics of his county. He was Justice of the Peace, at Ovid, one term, and served as District Attorney of Seneca County for two full terms, and was elected to his present position over Isaac N. Johnson, Republican. He has proved himself to be a most efficient member of the important Committees on Canals and Local and Special Laws, and has been assiduous and punctual in his attendance at the House.

Mr. Hazelton is quiet and unostentatious in his demeanor, and what he advocates is done effectively, but quietly. He is a plain, straight-forward speaker, and what he says is emphatic and to the purpose.

AUSTIN W. HOLDEN.

Mr. Holden, the efficient member from Warren County, was born at White Creek, Washington County, N. Y., May 16, 1819. He received his education at the Primary and District Schools, at the St. Lawrence Academy and at the Albany Medical College, and has been connected in various pursuits in life; first as cabinet-maker, then as teacher, and lastly as physician of the Homœopathic school. At the commencement of the war, Mr. Holden went to the front and served in various capacities; first as Captain and latterly as

Medical Officer on the staff, earning for himself a record of which he may justly be proud.

In politics Mr. Holden has been a life-long Democrat, but never an extremist. He has held the following positions: In 1846 and 1847 he was County Superintendent of Public Schools; was Coroner for several terms for the County of Warren; President of the Board of Health for Glen's Falls for the last three years; Trustee and Secretary of Glen's Falls Academy; corresponding or honorary member of various learned and scientific societies.

Mr. Holden was elected to his present seat in the Assembly, by a majority of sixty-two over Joseph Woodward, a prominent Republican candidate. In 1872 the Republican ticket received a majority of 1,000, thus showing the esteem in which the doctor is held in his district.

As an orator Dr. H. has not especially signalized himself, but that he possesses some ability in that direction, as well as sound judgment, there is no mistake, for on more than one occasion he has taken the floor and shown the earnestness and liberality of his views. What he has to say, he says briefly and to the purpose. As a worker he ,has few equals, for he has not been absent from his seat a single session. He is a member of the Committees on " Public Printing " and " Civil Divisions," and has faithfully discharged his duties in those relations. He was prominently identified with the educational bills favoring the Academy Appropriation in the Supply Bill, and making a speech thereon. He has also advocated several local measures in brief and pertinent remarks, so far having been successful in most of his undertakings in the House.

ERASTUS H. HUSSEY.

The member from Cayuga County can well be styled one of the solid men of the present Assembly, for one has but to look on the genial, good-natured countenance of Mr. Hussey and be satisfied that he is an honest, upright man. Quiet and

3

unassuming in his demeanor, he is a keen observer, and is as well posted on public affairs as any member in the House. Although he has not made himself conspicuous by speech-making, he has done so by the sound judgment he has displayed by his votes, and the punctuality of his attendance in the House as well as the efficient services he has rendered as a member of the Committee on Villages and Trades and Manufactures. Mr. Hussey was born in Ledyard, Cayuga County, January 19, 1827, where he received a good common-school and academic education, and he is now engaged in farming operations. He has been a member of the Board of Supervisors of his county since the year 1867. He was elected to his present seat by a majority of 1,292 over E. T. Brown, Democrat, and W. H. Manchester, Temperance.

Mr. LINCOLN,

Of Ontario.—One would take Mr. Cyrillo S. Lincoln for a public man and a statesman when seen. He has the appearance of a politician of the better class, and as such must be regarded. His massive head and long, flowing beard readily attract the stranger to inquire who he is, while his physiognomy indicates a good deal of force of character, and shows him to be a man of more than ordinary ability. And so he is, Mr. Lincoln being one of the decided lights of the present Legislature. He is an ardent and active partizan, who has strong notions of party fealty, and who never yet kicked in the traces. There is a courteousness of manner and frankness of language in all his political endeavors which invariably attracts admiration and respect from his most decided opponents. Exceedingly fluent in debate, he is unquestionably among the foremost members of the House, and is so regarded, having the important Chairmanship of Railroads given to his care and keeping. In this position he has been exposed to adverse and unwarranted criticisms, which, now that the session is at an end, are ascertained to have been utterly without foundation, but caused by petty jealousy and

personal feeling. Mr. Lincoln has fully vindicated himself
from the ungenerous slurs cast upon him, and leaves the
Assembly chamber this winter carrying with him the esteem
and admiration of every member upon the floor. Mr. Lincoln was born in this State in July, 1833. He received a
good education, studied law, and was admitted to practice.
He has served three consecutive terms in the Assembly, and
was prominently mentioned for Speaker at the opening of the
present session, but declined to allow his name to be used.

AUSTIN LEAKE.

Mr. Leake, who represents the Fifth district of New York,
is a man justly calculated to take good care of the interests
of his constituents, having lived nearly all his life in the
metropolis.   He was born in New York City, October 2, 1833;
received his education in the common schools, and, at an
early age, learned the trade of a sailmaker, but has left his
trade and is now engaged in the undertaking and livery business; moved to Pleasant Valley, Dutchess County, in 1866; was
elected Justice of the Peace the following year, resigning the
position amid the regrets of his neighbors, returned to New
York and engaged in the undertaking and livery business in
1869.

He has earnestly opposed the system of governing that
city by commissions, and has struggled earnestly to secure
that people the right of local self-government.   In politics
Mr. L. is a Republican, and he has always taken a deep interest in the politics of the State and country at large, but has
never before held any political office.   He was elected to the
present Assembly by a plurality vote of 806 over George L.
Loutrel, Tammany Democrat, and Arthur J. Delancy, Apollo
Democrat, and is assigned, as a member, to the important
Committees on Banks, Privileges and Elections and Sub-
Committee of the Whole.   He has been most earnest and
assiduous in his duties both in the committee-rooms and in

the House, and is recognized as a Legislator of the highest and purest character.

Mr. Leake has taken the floor on several occasions, and expressed his views distinctly and fearlessly. What he has to say is done on the spur of the moment, and, although the words are well weighed and to the purpose, he can lay no claim to oratory, but he invariably carries any measures that he advocates. He has been interested in the following bills: Making the office of Comptroller elective, Canal Enlargement, and whatever tended to increase the prosperity of the city and State.

HENRY LAWRENCE.

If travel and a thorough insight into the institutions both abroad and at home, contribute to a man's ability and experience, necessary for a Legislator, the gentleman who represents the First District of Columbia must indeed be a man of decided ability and experience ; for Mr. Henry Lawrence, of Claverack, has visited nearly every country on the globe in his capacity as a marine engineer.

Mr. Lawrence was born in New York city, October 15, 1825, where he received a good education in the common schools and became a marine engineer, and, after following his roving profession for thirty years, he retired to Claverack, where he now resides, and opened a hotel. In politics, Mr. Lawrence is a Democrat, and he has, of late years, taken an active part in politics, but has never before held office. He was elected to his present seat by a majority of 334 over Mr. John D. Langdon, Republican. He has done signal service as member of the Committees on Expenditures of the Executive Department and Public Lands, and has been most punctual in his attendance in the House.

Mr. Lawrence has not made himself conspicuous through speech-making, but by close observation it has been seen that he has, by his constant application to the business of the House, made himself worthy of a complimentary notice.

JEROME B. LANDFIELD.

Mr. Landfield may be styled a vetern politician, if we judge by the many positions that he has filled, although he is now but in his forty-seventh year. He is postmaster of Newark Valley, a town in which he is extensively engaged in mercantile pursuits, and has also been a member of the Tioga County Board of Supervisors for several years. He represented Delaware County in the Assembly in 1864, and Tioga County in 1872, when he made a good record as a member of the Committees on Railroads and Trade and Manufactures. He was elected to the present House, by a majority of 608, over Isaac S. Stanclift, Democrat. He is an earnest worker on the Committees on Railroads, Trade and Manufactures and State Prisons, and during the present session has been punctual in his attendance at the House. He is curt and pointed in his remarks, and although by no means an orator, he has been most successful in carrying the measures he has had in hand. During the present session, Mr. Landfield has displayed remarkable ability as a legislator. Crude and corrupt legislation has been strenuously opposed by him, while his voice has ever been raised on the side of honesty and good government. He has shown himself one of the ablest members on the floor, and commands the respect and esteem of all.

DANIEL P. McQUEEN.

Mr. McQueen, the good-looking member from Schenectady, is of Scotch origin and was born in Stockbridge, Mass., July 6, 1843, but was brought up in Schenectady where his father removed about twenty-five years ago. He was educated in the common schools and became, as his father was before him, a practical machinist and locomotive engineer.

Mr. McQueen has never held any political office prior to his election to his present position, nor indeed has he been much associated with politics, but such was his popularity at home that, in 1872, he was nominated by acclamation and

3*

elected by a majority of 489 over Thomas B. Mitchell, Democrat, and last year was re-elected by 154, over Arthur W. Hunter, a very powerful Democrat. Mr. McQueen, has been a hard worker and faithful in discharging his duties both in the House and in the Committee-rooms as Chairman of Federal Relations and member of Committee on Public Printing. Although not given to much speech making, Mr. McQueen has, on several occasions, addressed the House on bills when in Committee of the Whole. He is very brief and distinct in what he has to say and has accomplished more by acting than talking.

THEODORE N. MELVIN.

The County of Kings has long been noted for sending good and sound representatives to the Assembly, but in no year have the people of the Fourth district been so fortunate in their choice as when they sent the young, able lawyer, Mr. Melvin, to represent their interests in the House.

Although this is the first political office that Mr. Melvin has held, he at once rushed to the front and has earned for himself a good record as a public speaker and a Legislator of good sound judgment and probity. He has taken the floor on several occasions on very important questions pertaining to the interests of New York city and Brooklyn, and has expressed his views in somewhat lengthy but very able speeches. Mr. Melvin is a Democrat, and was elected to his present seat by a plurality of 822 over three opponents, one Republican and two Democrats.

He was born in New York city December 1, 1846, and received his education in the common schools. He studied law with Hon. J. S. Lawrence, was admitted to the Bar in 1868, and has a good practice in Brooklyn in partnership with ex-Judge W. Henry Gale.

Mr. PRINCE,

Of Queens.—A sleek, affable and modest-appearing gentleman is Mr. L. Bradford Prince, of Queens, a prominent candidate for Speaker at the beginning of the present session, and, at present, Chairman of the highly important Committee on Judiciary. He is not a new member by any means; for four years he has visited Albany as a Legislator, and has made during that time a very enviable record. It is evident that Mr. Prince has a fondness for purple and fine linen. That his tendencies are aristocratic, and that he would adorn the Senate chamber with even more happiness than the popular branch of the Legislature is quite apparent. He is an exceedingly talented man, studious, polite and friendly. He is regarded among his brother members as a keen observer, a rapid reasoner and an active thinker, worthy of occupying more exalted places of trust than he has yet been called to fill. His disposition is unruffled at all times, his social qualities elegant but cold, although to the ladies who, at times, grace, with their presence, the rear of the Senate chamber, Mr. Prince is regarded as a charming controversialist, and of many pleasant attributes. He is a gentleman who makes friends slowly, but who retains them at all times afterward.

Mr. Prince was born in Flushing, his present home, July 3, 1840, where he received a highly classical education, and, imbibing a taste for the legal profession, he entered Columbia Law College, and graduated from there with great honor. As a lawyer, he enjoys an enviable reputation, and his political career extends over a period of sixteen years. He has been the President of the Republican Committee of Queens County for several years, and he was also a delegate to the Chicago National Convention in 1868. He was first elected to the Assembly in 1870, since which time he has been re-elected three times. It is unnecessary to dwell on the legislative career of a gentleman of so wide a reputation; suffice it to say that throughout all his public life Mr. Prince has preserved an unsullied record. Besides being a prominent member of the Masonic fraternity, he is president and member of several scientific and learned societies.

EDWARD C. PHILPOT.

The First district of Madison County is fortunate indeed in being represented by so substantial and solid a man as Edward C. Philpot, who is now here for his second term. He was born in the town of Eaton, Madison County, November 9, 1834; was liberally educated in the common schools and at the Central New York Conference Seminary at Cazenovia, and, imbibing a taste for the legal profession, he studied law in the offices of Hon. Henry Goodwin and D. J. Mitchell, of Hamilton, and was admitted to the Bar in 1856, but he has never made the practice of his profession a speciality, except at one or two intervals, his agricultural and other interests having greater claims upon his attention.

Mr. Philpot has mingled largely in the local politics of his county, and his native town has honored him with every office within its gift—Justice of Peace, Justice of Sessions and Supervisor; and he was also a member of the last Legislature, serving as Chairman of the Committee on Petitions of Aliens, and member of Committee on Privileges and Elections, and earning for himself the record of a sound and honest legislator. His district has never returned a member the second term, but last fall Mr. Philpot was re-nominated by acclamation, and elected, by a majority of 1,000 votes, to the present Assembly. He has been assigned the Chairmanship of the Committee on Agriculture, and is a member of Committee on Civil Divisions, on which Committees he is a hard and zealous worker.

Mr. Philpot speaks but seldom, but for effective work he yields to none; is always in his seat attending to the business of the House, and watching closely the interests of his constituents.

NATHAN D. PETTY.

There is not a member who has more right to a prominent place in this book than Mr. Petty, for, although his advent in the Assembly chamber is his first step in legislative experience, he has already made himself conspicuous by the ability he has displayed in grappling the intricate and knotty questions of the State.

Mr. Petty was born in Goodground, Suffolk county, on January 6, 1842, and, after graduating with high honors from Princeton College, he entered the Law School in Albany, was admitted to the Bar in 1866, and commenced the practice of the law at Riverhead. Embracing the Republican principles firmly, he early showed a desire for politics, but did not accept any office, with the exception of Assistant Assessor of Internal Revenue for Suffolk County, which position he held until the office was abolished in 1873. He was elected to his present seat by a majority of 1,199 over Wilson J. Terry, Democrat, and Edward Y. Reeve, Prohibition. He is member of the Judiciary Committee, Grievances, and Local and Special Laws.

As a debater he is deserving of a foremost place. His reasoning is invariably sound and correct; his enunciation clear and distinct, and his language well chosen and indicative of a sound, cultivated mind. He only takes the floor when he is thoroughly conversant with the subject under consideration, and his views are invariably sound and weighty.

The first speech made by Mr. Petty, in the Assembly, was against the act to dissolve the Narrowsburgh Home Association. He opposed its passage on the ground that it was the worst kind of special legislation, as the relief asked for could be attained under existing general law. It passed the House but was killed in Senate. His next effort was in the great debate on the question of submitting the Proposed Amendment to Article Five of the Constitution to the people. He took the position that it should be submitted to the people for

their decision, but the vote in the House was against its sub-
mission.   His next speech was against the act in relation to
County Treasurers, claiming that some of its provisions were
unconstitutional.   It passed the House, but those provisions
were stricken out in the Senate.

His greatest effort and speech was made on March 24th, in
favor of Compulsory Education.   The act passed the Assembly by a large majority.

The next speech that attracted attention was one made in
joint caucus of Senate and Assembly, in putting Addison A.
Keyes, of Albany, in nomination for Superintendent of Public Instruction.   The speech was as follows :

*Speech of Hon. N. D. Petty, of Suffolk, in joint
caucus of the Senate and Assembly, April 6th,
1874, nominating Addison A. Keyes for Superintendent of Public Instruction.*

Mr. CHAIRMAN.—Rising, as I do, to name a candidate for
Superintendent of Public Instruction, I desire to present to
this caucus the name of a gentleman well known to the
people of this State as being one eminently fitted for the
position, from his long experience in the Department of Public Instruction, and in general school matters.   He is a native
of Chautauqua County and at present a resident of this city;
a graduate of the Law University of Albany, and a member
of the Bar of this State, possessing in a high degree that
legal knowledge so desirable in this department.   He has
been connected with the State Department of Public Instruction since 1865.   Under Superintendent Rice, he had the
entire charge of the most important bureau in the department, that of correspondence and appeals.   He had charge
of all appeal cases, for three years, under Mr. Rice, and for
one year and a half under Superintendent Weaver; his legal
attainments enabling him to discharge the duties of that
bureau faithfully and well, and to the entire satisfaction of
both Superintendents.   For some years past he has been a
member of the school board in Albany, and is now President of that board.   He is also one of the editors of a
prominent and influential Republican journal, that has done
good service, and has accomplished much, for our party.   In
the editorial chair he has distinguished himself with great
ability as a writer, and has ever stood firm to principle and
to the great Republican party.

Through the columns of that paper he has always vindicated the progressive ideas of his party and its broad and
mighty principles.

Last, but not least, when the war came, when the nation
was bleeding at every pore, when the cry for help came,
and when the Government appealed to the heroism of its
sons, it was the one I am about to nominate, who went to
the front for three and a half years as an officer, fought our
battles, protected our flag, and aided, by his strong arm, in
retaining the thick clustering stars of that tri-colored emblem
in one glorious constellation forever.

He has claims on this caucus that it cannot overlook or
disregard. He has honored his country; let his country
honor him.

Mr. Chairman, it is with pleasure that I nominate for
Superintendent of Public Instruction, Addison A. Keyes of
the city of Albany.

Besides many other bills of a local nature, effecting only
his own county, he has rendered invaluable service to his
party as a speaker ; stumping, as he has, the States of New
York and New Jersey in every Presidential and Gubernato-
rial canvass from 1864.

CHARLES S. SPENCER.

The gentleman best known on the floor of the Assembly
chamber this winter, and the one to whom all are friendly
and who is friendly to all, is the eminently popular member
from the Thirteenth Metropolitan District, the Hon. Charles
Spencer, of New York. As a great criminal lawyer and an
earnest, forcible advocate, his fame long ago extended
throughout the State, and this winter he has but added lustre
to a reputation well earned and brilliant. Few men are
blessed with the many attributes of success Mr. Spencer is possessed of ; few are fortunate enough to have so kindly and generous a nature as to win such popularity and universal esteem.
It is, perhaps, needless for us to recount the triumphs of this
gentleman during the present winter ; they have been con-
tinuous and successive, and we fail to recollect a single measure in which he has been unsuccessful. He it was who

championed the opposition to the famous Fifth Article of the Proposed Amendments to the Constitution, holding it to be in direct antagonism to the rights of the people. The Assembly was apparently opposed to his views, but, with matchless eloquence and rare power, he spoke for the whole people and carried his point ; the article was defeated. This is but one of his triumphs. So kindly is the nature of this exceedingly estimable gentleman, that he is constantly doing good and casting sunshine and happiness about him. A young man, who had suffered the pangs of adversity, was recently arrested on the charge of securing food for his family through false pretences. It came to the ears of " Charley " Spencer, the poor man's friend ; he ascertained that the young man was not really dishonest, but very unfortunate; at once he went to the court-room, became his counsel, and, after an eloquent plea, secured the discharge of the poor fellow—a perfect stranger—and sent him on his way rejoicing. Graceful acts of generosity and humanity, such as these, are of repeated occurrence. His heart is as open as the sea, his generosity as boundless, and to the humblest page-boy on the floor he is as kindly and courteous as to the wealthiest of his constituents. A man of prepossessing appearance, with a bright, merry twinkle in his eye, his person, as well as his genial manners, attract. Mr. Spencer's instincts and sympathies are all with the people, and opposed to aristocratic monopolies. He is ever anxious to confer benefits upon the industrial classes, and, by his public-spirited liberality, has rendered himself so exceedingly popular. On the floor of the House he excels as a debater, his wit is as keen as a Damascus blade, his oratory is of that pleasing, convincing style, which wins as well as delights; a member of unswerving activity, energy and perseverence, he represents, with ability and honor, his constituency. Though he always speaks extemporaneously, and often without preparation, his efforts are generally models of compact, symmetrical argument. Indeed, we can truly say of Mr. Spencer, whether we regard him in his private or public life, that he is above reproach, and is, in all respects, an honest, able and efficient Legislator. A staunch Republican he has ever been, and is unfaltering in his devotion to his country, his party and his friends. Mr. Spencer was born in Ithaca, this State, in February, 1824, was married in 1849, to Miss Loomis, of Auburn, who, during the present winter, has presided over Mr. Spencer's elegant mansion, with all the grace and charm of the cultivated, estimable lady that she is. The receptions given by Col. and Mrs. Spencer this winter, have been the most brilliant and successful of the season, and the end of the session is, consequently, regretted by the *elite* of Albany society. It is safe to say that the most prominent member of the present Legislature is the subject of this sketch, Charles S. Spencer of New York.

GEORGE B. SLOAN.

Mr. Sloan, the quiet but gentlemanly representative from the First district of Oswego, was born in Oswego, June 20, 1832, where he received a good common-school education, and early embarked in commercial pursuits which he has followed with much success, and has now established the well-known grain firm of Erwin & Sloan.

Although Mr. Sloan is held in the highest esteem by his fellow-citizens he has persistently refused to accept any political office, but he was constrained to accept his present position as he was unanimously nominated by the Republican District Convention, and he was elected by a majority of 1,200 over Mr. Fort, Democrat.

Mr. Sloan has taken the floor on several occasions and made some very able remarks on measures pertaining principally to Education and Canals, on which subjects he is perfectly at home and conversant. He also delivered a very eloquent address on the occasion of the death of Senator Sumner; but generally, the gentleman's speeches are characteristic of the man—short, pithy and logical. Mr. Sloan has made an excellent record this winter, having been very

4

punctual and assiduous in his duties, both in the House and
Committee-room.

GEORGE SHERWOOD.

The voters of Broome County were indeed happy in their
choice when they sent Mr. George Sherwood to represent their
interests in the Assembly, for not only have their interests been
ably looked after but the monotony of the House has also
been pleasantly disturbed by the à *propos* and instructive
stories and anecdotes that have been used by the veteran
from Broome when speaking against or advocating any bill.

Mr. Sherwood has been most active in opposing any
unnecessary expenditure of money, and his speeches are
invariably on the side of purity and righteousness, or in favor
of temperance, and in every speech he is sure to bring in
some story or anecdote so justly appropriate and applicable
to the question at issue that he is certain to carry his measure.
He is quaintly original in his style of speaking, reminding
one somewhat of a Methodist at a revival, but as soon as the
gentleman rises he is listened to more attentively than any
other member of the House, and invariably he sets the members in roars of laughter.

Mr. Sherwood is a Republican in politics and, although
he has never sought for any political honors, he was elected
in 1870 a member of the Board of Supervisors from Binghamton.

Mr. S. was born at McDonough's Springs, Chenango
County, January 18, 1820, and can be termed a self educated
man, having only attended school for a very short time, but
there is no mistake but that he is a well-informed man, and,
although some may deem him a " one idea " man, his views
are sound and logical.

The following are the principal measures advocated by Mr.
Sherwood: The bills for Susquehanna River Bridges; Ruloff
Reward; Building Bell over Fireman's Hall, Binghamton;
Cemetery and Public Park, Binghamton; Additional Police,

Binghamton; Sewerage in Binghamton; Susquehanna Valley Home; Extending the time to Collect Taxes in Whitney's Point; $5,000 for Repairs to River Bank.

FREDERICK SCHIFFERDECKER.

Mr. Schifferdecker, the subject of the present sketch, was born in Baden, Germany, February 2, 1836, and was brought to this country, by his father, at the outburst of the revolution in that country in 1848, who left behind him extensive landed property, being a man of considerable means. The younger Schifferdecker received his education in the German common schools, and he early evinced a spirit of independence, for he commenced work at a furnace at the small stipend of seventy-five cents a week, and, after trying his fortune at various other employments, he embarked in the meat business. Soon after the civil war commenced, and the characteristic warlike spirit of the Schifferdeckers was roused, the subject of our sketch went eagerly to the front and served his adopted country in a manner not surpassed by any of her own legitimate sons. He was wounded in more than one engagement, and he still bears the scars of his wounds. His army record is one that he may justly be proud of, and which should entitle him to the worthy consideration of every true American. He left the army, after the termination of the war, with the rank of Captain, and entered once more into the meat business, which he has since carried on with such success as to place him in comfortable circumstances.

In politics Mr. Schifferdecker is a Republican, and he has upheld those principles for the last eighteen years and done considerable service to his party. He has not been a seeker after political offices, but he was elected a member of the Board of Supervisors in 1870 and 1871, and his record during the tenure of those offices was such as to convince his constituents that he was a good, honest and zealous public servant, and last fall he was elected over Barent S. Winne, a popular and powerful Democrat, to the Assembly, and well indeed has he carried out the duties assigned him. As a working member of the Committees on Two-thirds and Three-fifths bills, Expenditures of the Executive Department and Expenditures of the House, he has no superior. He has been most punctual in his attendance at the House, and indefatigable in his endeavors to pass the bills confided to him and looking after the interests of his constituents. His principal aim has been to pass a law that would destroy the monopoly of the Gas Companies of Albany, and should he not succeed it will not be owing to his exertions, but to a want of outside co-operation.

Although not aspiring to oratorical honors, Mr. S. has given his views on several questions in brief but pointed language. By his frank and open deportment, and genial, generous nature, he has made himself a general favorite in the House.

MARTIN L. STOVER.

Mr. Stover, who has entered the political arena for the first time, was born in Waterloo, N. Y., October 19th, 1845. He was educated at Wittenburg College, Springfield, Ohio ; was admitted to the Bar in 1870, and then removed to Amsterdam, where he enjoys a good practice. He has always been an adherent to Republican principles, and was elected to the present Assembly, over Hon. Isaac S. Frost, Democrat, by a fair majority.

Mr. Stover is a member of the Committees on Railroads, Federal Relations and Public Lands, and has been most assiduous in his duties on the Committees. He is rarely absent from his seat in the House, and although he does not rank as an orator, he has urged the passage of local bills connected with his district in brief but matter of fact speeches.

ROBERT A. SNYDER.

Few members of the Assembly are held in such high esteem as the worthy member for the First district of Ulster County, Mr. Robert A. Snyder. He is a valuable man in all the details of legislation, as well as in the Committee-room, where he has earned a good record as a member of the Committees on Commerce and Navigation and Federal Relations. Although not given to much speech-making, he has, on several occasions, taken the floor and expressed his views in brief but pointed language.

Mr. Snyder was born in the city of Poughkeepsie, May 18, 1836, where he received a good common-school education and embarked, at an early age, in business pursuits. He was married on the 5th of March, 1863, to Miss Jane S. Morgan, at Catskill, and then removed to Saugerties, where he embarked in the transportation business.

In politics Mr. S. is an ardent Republican and has done considerable service for his party, but has never been an aspirant for public honors. In 1870 he was elected Collector of the town of Saugerties, and last year represented the same town in the Board of Supervisors. He was elected to his present seat by a majority of 1,170 over Peter Gile, a powerful Democrat.

SAMUEL W. TEWKSBURY.

Wyoming County has a good, substantial representative, this year, in the person of Mr. Tewksbury, who is worthy of notice, not from any eloquent outburst of oratory, for he is a man of few words, but from the earnestness and perseverance he has displayed in catering to the wants and interests of his constituency, and for his punctuality of attendance, both in the House and the Committee-room. Although he has been more or less connected with politics all his life, he has preserved the record of an upright and incorruptible man.

4*

Mr. Tewksbury was born in York, Livingston County, July 23, 1820, of New England parentage, and he received a good common-school and academic education. He taught school for some years, and finally purchased the farm on which he now resides. In politics Mr. T. is an unswerving Republican, and, during a period of eleven years, he was elected Town Superintendent of Common Schools, and, five times, he was Justice of the Peace, and, during six years, he has represented his town in the Board of Supervisors. He was, also, a delegate from Wyoming County at the exciting Republican State Conventions in 1868 and 1872, and in all these numerous capacities, he has always sought to perform his duties with a watchful eye to the public weal, and he now leaves the Assembly chamber with a record untarnished, but with increased popularity. He is a member of the Committees on Charitable and Religious Societies and Agriculture.

COMMODORE P. VEDDER.

The gentleman who represents Cattaraugus County in the present Assembly is confessedly one of the brightest ornaments of the Legislature of 1874. Capable, efficient, and eloquent are terms truly applicable to him, and but express the elements which predominate in him. He is a comparatively young man, of exceeding merit, and is regarded by his fellow-members as the personification of honor, integrity and good nature. He speaks admirably, addressing the House with a force and finish peculiarly his own, and which is, generally, immediately effective. He is outspoken and fearless; condemns a measure unsparingly if, in his judgment, it is in opposition to the people's interest, but advocates warmly a bill of merit. Mr. Vedder has been a soldier and a sailor, and is now a lawyer of celebrity and a Legislator of mark, who, for the good of the whole people, we hope to have among us again.

SMITH M. WEED,

Of Clinton.—From the forest of Clinton County comes Smith M. Weed, a gentleman well known throughout the length and breadth of the State as a politician of prominence, a lawyer of celebrity, and a scholar of exceeding culture. For the last decade of years Mr. Weed has been a leading man in northern New York—not only in its politics but in its vast business interests, with which he is closely connected.

But he is a man who looks beyond the interests of localities, and who is sound on any great question that arises affecting the whole commonwealth. A speaker of care and much deliberation his words are weighty, but few; his arguments being generally logical and convincing. During this session and the last one Mr. Weed has been especially prominent in the character of the legislation he has advocated. During last winter he earnestly advocated the passage of the Champlain Ship Canal bill, and secured its passage through the Assembly. This year he most distinguished himself by opposing the Fifth Article of the Proposed Constitutional Amendment—the defeat of which is mainly due to his efforts. Indeed, had it not been for Mr. Weed's efforts in that direction, the article, which certainly had a tendency to concentrate and centralize power which belongs to the people, would have been adopted. Mr. Weed is one of the finest looking men in the House; of medium stature, his robust form and broad shoulders seem well able to carry the massive and well-developed head which is a fit repository for a brain of more than ordinary activity. His dark flowing beard and piercing black eyes make him conspicuous in the chamber in which he is one of the brightest lights. Mr. Weed was born in Franklin County July, 1833. He was educated at Harvard and was married to an estimable lady, a lineal descendant of Miles Standish, in 1859. He was a member of the Constitutional Convention of 1867, a Member of Assembly for several years, where he has twice been honored with being the candidate of his party for Speaker. His reputation continues to enlarge itself, and a brilliant future seems promised to Mr. Smith M. Weed.

GEORGE WEST.

The career of this gentleman is a fair example of what energy, sagacity and persevering industry can accomplish. Mr. West was born in Kentisbere, Devonshire, England, February 17, 1823, and received a good common-school education, but finding that England did not afford scope enough for his expansive ideas, he emigrated to this country in 1849, and when he landed he was next to penniless, without any friends to help him; but with the indomitable pluck characteristic of his race, he obtained employment, and gradually bettering his condition, he removed to Ballston Spa, Saratoga county, and engaged in the paper manufacturing business, and he is at the present time sole proprietor of five large paper mills, which are run exclusively on Manilla paper. Mr. West is one of the wealthiest men in the House, and the fact that this is his third term in the Assembly, is a fair guarantee of the esteem and confidence in which he is held by his fellow-citizens. On the last two elections no competitor opposed him.

As a Legislator Mr. West is very cautious and extremely tenacious as to the interests of the manufacturers' rights and the interests of the working classes. He frequently addresses the House, when his speeches are characterized by wit and brevity. The Speaker was very happy in his choice when he assigned Mr. W. to the Chairmanship of the important Committee on Trades and Manufactures, for he is specially adapted for that office, and no member is better posted with the manufacturers' interests than he; he has also done good service as a member of the Committees on Public Printing and Public Lands. Mr. West is a good specimen of a sturdy Englishman, and though somewhat short in stature, he has a strong, heavy frame that seems capable of much endurance.

ALFRED WAGSTAFF, Jr.

Mr. Wagstaff, member from New York city, is recognized as the wit of the Assembly Chamber, and is one of the most popular men of the House. He has been a most active member, both in the House and in the Committee-room, and has frequently taken the floor, when he is certain to bring down the House by his ready remarks and repartees, as he possesses a keen sense of the ludicrous as well as substantial facts.

Mr. Wagstaff was born in New York city, of Anglo-Franco parentage, March 21, 1844, and received a highly classical education, and, in 1866, graduated from Columbia College Law School, with the degree of L. L. B., and at once commenced the practice of his profession in the metropolis.

He served through the war, holding various positions and making a good record, and retired with the rank of Lieutenant-Colonel. On Governor Fenton's election, he appointed the Colonel aid-de-camp on his staff. Colonel Wagstaff has been associated with politics since 1866, when he was a delegate to the Republican Convention at Syracuse, and was one of the vice-presidents of that body, and, in the fall of the same year, he was elected to the Assembly, by a majority of 486. Since then he has been a delegate to several political conventions and bodies, and otherwise identified with the political movements of New York city. In 1872, Colonel Wagstaff joined the Liberal Republican ranks, and was elected by them to his present position, by a majority of 239.

AMHERST WIGHT, Jr.

Amiable, unpretending in every respect, Mr. Wight has gained much popularity during his sojourn in Albany this winter, and excellent service has been accomplished by him for the people of Westchester County. He is always to be found in his seat, and is also punctual in his attendance in the Committee-room. He was assigned, the present session, to the Chairmanship of the important Committee on Insurance, and is also a member of Judiciary and Sub-Committee of the Whole.

Mr. Wight has, on several occasions, taken the floor and spoken on important matters and expressed his views briefly and logically, making use of graceful and appropriate language. His addresses on the death of Senator Sumner and also the late Mr. Knapp were, indeed, evidences of a well-cultured and highly educated mind.

Mr. Wight was born in New York city, August 15, 1828 and he learned the first rudiments of his education in a private school, after which he applied himself vigorously to the study of the classics. He studied law, and, on coming of age, was admitted to the Bar, and now enjoys a lucrative practice in the courts of New York and Westchester. Mr. Wight has never taken a very active part in politics, but has always had a deep feeling of interest in the fortunes of the Republican party. In 1871 and 1872 he represented the town of Portchester in the Board of Supervisors, and, in 1872, he defeated Elias Dusenbury, by a small majority, for the Assembly. Last fall he was re-elected over John H. Cornell, Democrat, by a majority of ninety-three.

CHARLES B. WOOD.

Major Chas. B. Wood, member from the Second District of Orange County, is a young man of much promise and has proved himself to be a hard worker, although a silent member, but he is always to be found in his seat where he is often consulted by other members on measures pertaining to his party. He has alike been faithful in the discharge of his duties both in the House and in the committee-room where he serves as a member of the Committees on Two-thirds and Three-fifths Bills and Indian Affairs.

Mr. Wood was born at Warwick, Orange County, September 3, 1837, and was educated in the public schools, and

shortly after leaving which he engaged in railroading, and he
is now conductor on the Erie Railway. Mr. W.'s army record
is such as he may justly be proud of. He entered the army
as a private and left as Captain, disabled from wounds received
while in action, and was afterward breveted Major for meri-
torious and gallant conduct during the war. In politics the
Major is a strict Democrat, and although he has always taken
a deep interest in political matters, he has never before
accepted any office. He was elected to his seat by a majority
of 892 over Benjamin F. Bailey, Republican.

PETER WOODS.

This gentleman who ably represents the Sixteenth district
of New York city, can safely be styled the Champion of the
Laboring Classes, for he is in deep sympathy with those who
earn their bread by the sweat of their brow, being himself a
mechanic. In his endeavors to secure proper legislation to
reconcile the conflicting interests of capital and labor, Mr.
Woods made one of the most impassioned speeches of the
session, in the early part of the winter. He is a Democrat
of the order of " Young Democracy," but he has been a per-
sistent and bitter foe, for nine years, of Tammany Hall and
of all the schemes connected therewith. Mr. Woods is a
native of Ireland, but came to this country when quite
young. He is forty-one years old, has a stout short frame
and a pleasing countenance. Although for a long time identified with the politics of the city, Mr. W. never held any
office prior to being elected to the House in 1872. Last fall
he was re-elected on the Liberal-Republican ticket, over
Joseph B. Varnum, Republican and Nicholas Haughton,
Apollo Hall. Mr. Woods is a man of great business energy
and has been a hard worker in both the Committee-room
and House, but on certain occasions business has called him
to New York for a day or two at a time.

48 LIGHTS OF THE LEGISLATURE.

LOUIS C. WAEHNER.

The present Legislature has been somewhat remarkable for the fact that it has produced so many young members, who have at once rushed to the front and taken a foremost place in the ranks of oratory, and no member of the House is entitled to more consideration than the young member, Mr. Louis C. Waehner, who represents the Tenth district of New York city. That he has made an honorable record there is no disputing. He grapples the most knotty questions with the shrewdness and tenacity of an Alvord, and being a fluent and powerful speaker, he takes the floor upon almost every important question, especially when it touches the interests of his city, and has shown to the House that he possesses fine legal abilities and decision of character. He has a powerful resonant voice and a good delivery, and uses appropriate and graceful language, thereby entitling him to a prominent place among the orators of the Assembly Chamber.

Mr. Waehner is of German origin, and was born in New York city, where he received his education in the public schools. He studied law with Messrs. Stillwell & Swain of that city, and about six years ago he was admitted to the Bar, and now enjoys a lucrative practice. In politics he has always been a Democrat, and has taken an interest and been quite active in political campaigns, and, in 1872, while running as an Independent candidate, was defeated for the Assembly.